Solo Flyer

Story by Jackie Tidey
Illustrations by Trish Hill

NELSON PRICE MILBURN

"Have a good holiday," said Kel's mum,
as she waved goodbye to him at the airport.

"Bye, Mum," said Kel.
"I'll phone you tonight from Dad's place."

Kel lived with his mother,
but in the school holidays
he went to stay with his dad
who lived in another city.

Kel had to fly there
all by himself in a big jet.
He always wore a badge
that said:

Solo Flyer
Kel Ryan

Kel had travelled on his own many times, and he loved being on a plane.

After the flight, Kel was very pleased
to see his dad waiting for him in the crowd.
The airport was so busy and noisy.

"Hi, Dad!" Kel called as he raced over
to meet him.
"Look! I've got some new shoes,
and Mum bought me a great new bag, too."

"You are growing fast," said Dad.
"No wonder you needed new shoes.
Let's go and get your bag
so you can show that to me, too."

Kel's dad worked at the airport.
He was a baggage handler,
and he had just come off duty.

Kel and his dad walked to
the baggage claim area
with all the other passengers.
"There's Carousel 3," said Kel.

They stood and waited for Kel's bag
to come tumbling down the chute.
Then Dad noticed that
another carousel had stopped moving.
"Some bags must be stuck inside,"
he said to Kel.
"I'll just run over and help Jack clear it.
Wait here, Kel. I'll only be a minute."

But Kel was watching his new red bag
coming down the chute.
He didn't hear what his dad was saying.
He didn't see him hurry across
to the other carousel.

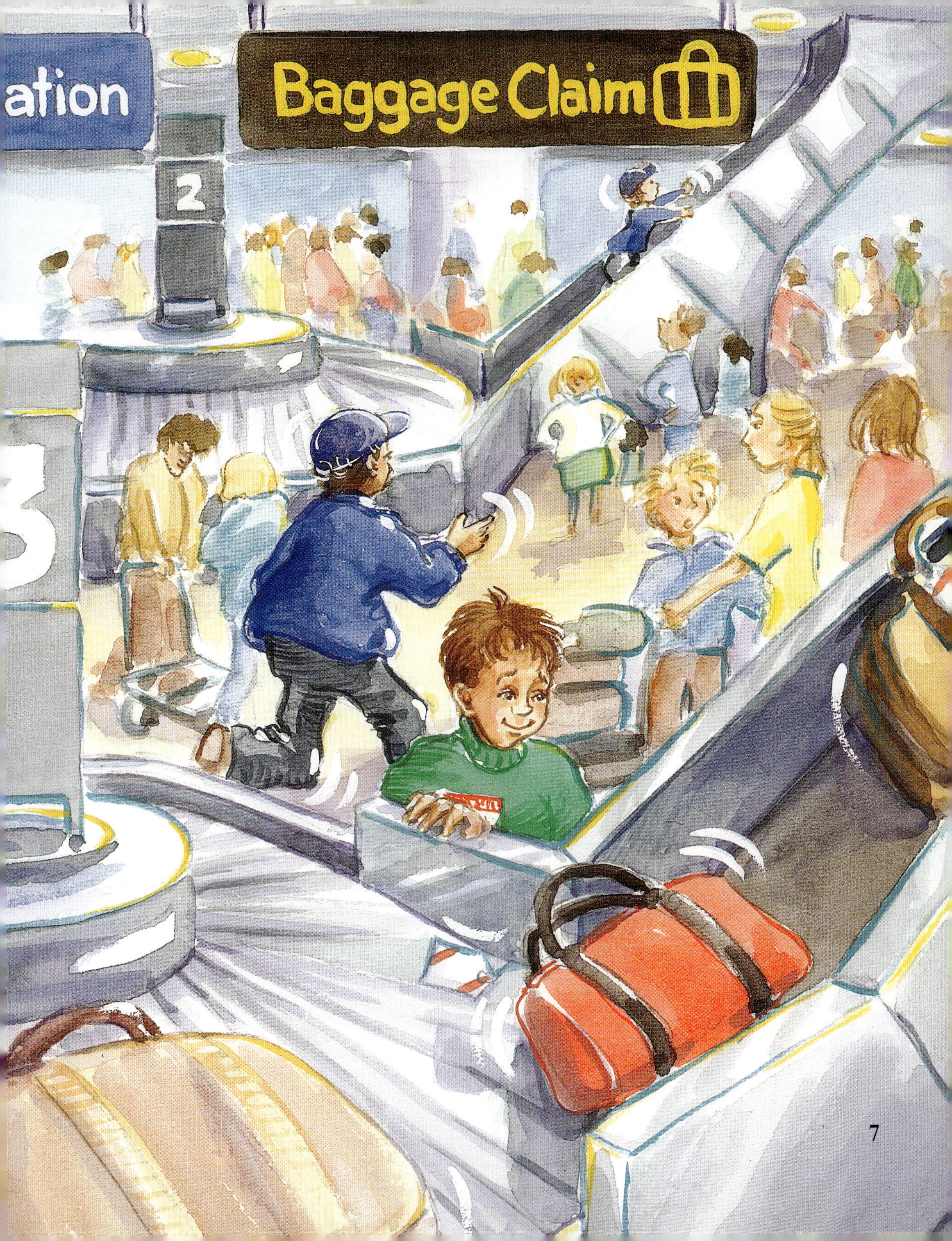
ation
Baggage Claim
2
3

Kel grabbed his bag as it was going past.
He turned to show it to his dad.
"Here's my new bag!" he said.
But his dad wasn't there.

Kel looked around.
He could see legs everywhere,
and lots of baggage,
but he couldn't see his dad.

Then he saw a man in an airport uniform
talking into a mobile phone.
"Oh, there he is," thought Kel,
and he ran across to him.
"Dad!" he called. "I've got my bag."
The man turned and looked down.

He was not Kel's dad, after all!

Kel rushed back to Carousel 3,
but his dad wasn't there, either.
Just for a minute Kel was very scared.
He tried not to panic.

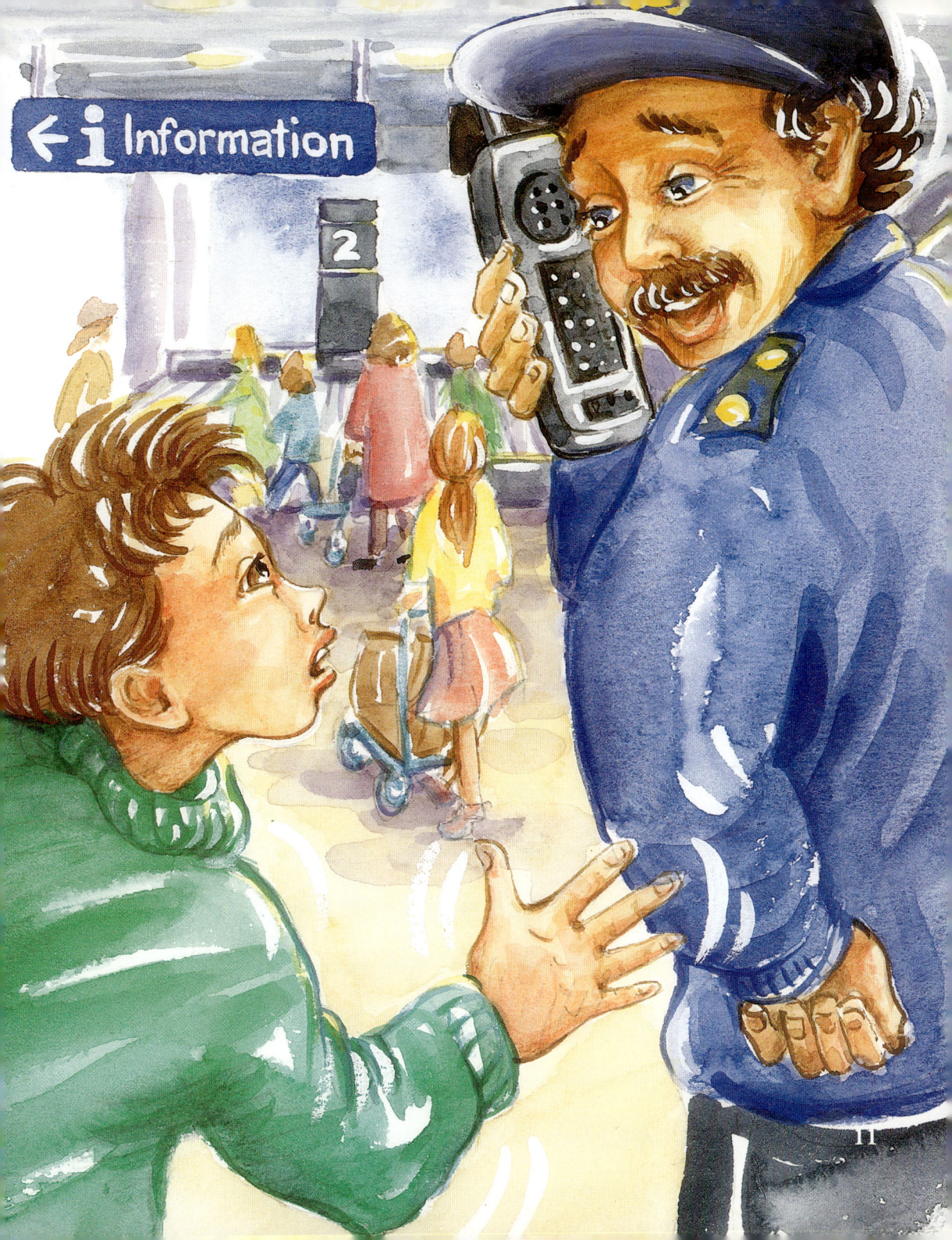

Information

Then Kel stopped to think.
He had been at this airport
many times before.
He took a deep breath
and looked up at the signs.

Kel knew what to look for:

← ⓘ Information

That was the sign he needed!

Kel went to the information desk.
He spoke to the woman behind the counter.
"I'm Kel Ryan and I want to find my dad.
His name is Tim Ryan and he works here.
Will you page him for me, please?"

The woman smiled and nodded to Kel.
"Wait here and I'll page your dad for you."
She spoke into her microphone
and her voice came over the loudspeaker.

**"Paging Tim Ryan. Paging Tim Ryan.
Please report to the information desk.
Your son is waiting for you."**

Kel looked around.
Suddenly he saw someone
waving above the crowd.
His dad was climbing out
of the top of the baggage chute,
and he was waving to Kel
from the other side of the hall!

Kel's dad ran down the chute
and started the carousel again.
Then he hurried over to Kel.

"I'm sorry I was away for so long," he said.
"It took longer to fix than I thought."
He put his arm around Kel.
"Hey! That **is** a great new bag.
Come on. I'm off duty. Let's go home."